Original title:
Creative Minds Unite

Editor: Jessica Elisabeth Luik
Author: Kaido Väinamäe
ISBN HARDBACK: 978-9916-86-246-9
ISBN PAPERBACK: 978-9916-86-247-6

Palettes of Innovation

In the heart of endless night,
Ideas spark, igniting flight,
Canvas fresh, a virgin white,
Dreams take shape, ignite the light.

Brush in hand, the future calls,
Breaking down the doubter's walls,
Colors blend as vision sprawls,
Creation's dance, where none yet stalls.

Harmony in fractured tones,
From the seed, the sapling grows,
In every shade, a journey shown,
The art of life, in flux, it flows.

Invention in each stroke displayed,
From chaos, order subtly made,
Boundaries in perceptions swayed,
Within the hues where thoughts cascade.

Every failure, a doorway wide,
Leading to the brighter side,
In palettes, where our hopes reside,
Innovation knows no tide.

Voices in Harmony

In the whisper of the wind, we find a song,
A chorus of souls, where we all belong.
Echoes of love in each gentle refrain,
Uniting hearts in joy and pain.

Harmonious threads weave through the night,
Guided by stars, so brilliantly bright.
Together in cadence, we rise and we fall,
Sharing the music that binds us all.

From dawn to dusk, and twilight's embrace,
Voices unite in a sacred space.
In every rhythm, a story unfolds,
A tapestry of life, rich and bold.

Elysian Epics

On fields of gold where dreams do tread,
Ancient tales of heroes spread.
In realms where mortals reach for skies,
Their epics etched in timeless eyes.

Zephyr's whispers tell the lore,
Of quests and love and battles' roar.
In shadow and in light, they roam,
Creating myths that speak of home.

Stars bear witness to their fate,
As legends grow and propagate.
In timeless dance, their lives entwine,
Elysian echoes through the spine.

Mosaic of Minds

Fragments of thought, so diverse, so vast,
In colors bright, they hold the past.
Each piece a story, unique and grand,
A mosaic of minds, by dreams planned.

Ideas clash and blend in light,
Forming visions, day and night.
In this dance of intellect,
New worlds and wonders intersect.

Through chaos, beauty finds its place,
In minds that seek the vastest space.
Unified yet brilliantly free,
A tapestry of thought we see.

Infinite Melodies

In the boundless stretch of time and space,
Melodies infinite find their grace.
Notes that travel on the winds of noon,
Harmonies born under the moon.

Ancient songs and future cries,
Blend in the symphony of the skies.
Every chord, a cosmic tale,
Infinite and never frail.

Strings of stars, a cosmic lyre,
Played by hands of endless fire.
In this music, life's rhythm flows,
Eternal echo that forever grows.

Dreamers' Constellation

Beneath a sky of velvet night,
A world of stars in pure delight.
Dreamers gaze with hearts so bright,
Mapping paths in cosmic flight.

Galaxies whisper ancient lore,
Infinite truths the skies implore.
In every twinkle, visions soar,
Endless dreams forevermore.

Constellations weave the tale,
Guiding ships with shimmering sail.
Through vast infinity, prevail,
Eclipsing doubts that may assail.

Silent songs of stars above,
Serenades of endless love.
Dreamers' hearts, the night will shove,
In constellations find their trove.

Rhapsody in Innovation

In the heart of minds that dare,
New ideas dance through the air.
Sparks ignite with brightened flair,
Innovation everywhere.

Creating paths unseen before,
Unlocking futures, open door.
Boundless realms we must explore,
New horizons to implore.

Progress sings a vibrant tune,
Underneath the guiding moon.
Every dawn, a different noon,
Innovations coming soon.

Boldly we design our fate,
In the crucible, create.
May our journeys resonate,
A rhapsody to celebrate.

Muses in Harmony

Muses whisper, soft and light,
Inspiration takes its flight.
Painted dreams in colors bright,
Art and song through endless night.

Voices blend in perfect key,
Weaving threads of unity.
Harmony in melody,
Creating timeless symphony.

Each note carries tales of old,
Every stroke a story told.
Hearts and souls in rhythms bold,
Muses' hands in art unfold.

From the silence, wonders rise,
In creations, seek the prize.
Musing with celestial ties,
Harmony that never dies.

Woven Whimsy

Threads of dreams we interlace,
In a tapestry of grace.
Woven tales from each embrace,
Patterned with a timeless pace.

Colors blend in playful dance,
Every strand creates a chance.
Whimsy found in each glance,
Life's creation at first glance.

Textures soft and stories vast,
Chapters in the loom are cast.
Woven past and futures fast,
Hearts entwined till bonds outlast.

In the fabric, joy ensues,
Magic found in varied hues.
Woven whimsy, dreams imbues,
A masterpiece that life renews.

Synchronic Inspirations

In moments where our minds align,
A spark ignites, a bright design.
Ideas dance, entwined in grace,
Creating wonders face to face.

Whispers shared in quiet air,
Magic born from what we dare.
Theory melds with purest art,
Heart to heart, an echoed start.

Threads of thought together weave,
Patterns none could hope conceive.
Each new line, a shared delight,
Lighting up the endless night.

Boundaries blur, and walls collapse,
New world maps from ancient scraps.
Inspiration flows, unchained,
Innovation, dreams sustained.

Uniting Forces of Innovation

Forces gather, none too small,
To breach the bounds, to leap, to fall.
United strength, a potent stream,
Transforms the world, fulfills the dream.

Vision shared by kindred souls,
Boundless hope that overflows.
New ideas, in tandem born,
Rip through dark, illuminate morn.

Harmony in flux, they blend,
Forge ahead, no need to mend.
Different minds, a single bent,
Destiny in pure consent.

In unity, we find our fire,
Fuel of fervent, grand desire.
Innovation's force revealed,
In combined hearts, our fate is sealed.

The Meeting of Minds

Beneath the sky, where thinkers meet,
Wisdom waits in clear retreat.
Minds converge, a subtle link,
Brewing thoughts from which we drink.

Cerebral dance, a gentle sway,
From dusk till dawn, ideas play.
Whispered theories, grand schemes born,
In intellect, the veil is torn.

Concepts merge in concert's thread,
Fuse in brilliance, light ahead.
From this circle, boundless case,
Infinite, the mapped out space.

Every thought, a precious bead,
Joined in strings of truth, indeed.
Fleeting moments, endless scope,
In minds we meet, we find our hope.

A Kaleidoscope of Genius

Splendor found in varied mind,
Wonder woven, thoughts aligned.
Color bursts and patterns, grand,
A genius touch in every hand.

Turn of glass, new visions spring,
Ideas fresh, in chorus sing.
Brilliance spins in vivid hues,
Wisdom shared in rainbow views.

Each new shard of insight gleams,
Flush with truth and vibrant dreams.
Kaleidoscopic lens of thought,
Finds the beauty life has brought.

Infinite, the shapes and forms,
Shift through storms and calmest norms.
Genius builds with each new spin,
Creating worlds from deep within.

Harmonic Horizons

On the edge of twilight's veil,
Whispering winds of time prevail,
Golden hues the sky adorn,
In dawn's light, we're reborn.

Stars dissolve in morning's grace,
Softly lights the world's embrace,
Horizons broad, profound, and near,
Future calls, the path is clear.

Echoes of the night subside,
As the day and dreams collide,
In the rhythm of the morn,
New harmonies are born.

Clouds in clusters gently part,
Reveal the canvas, nature's art,
With each pulse, life's song we chase,
In every heart, a tranquil space.

Brilliant Pulse

In the dance of light and dark,
Time leaves an indelible mark,
Moments flare like stars in flight,
Brilliant pulses in the night.

Through the curtain of the rain,
Colors flash and back again,
Life's heartbeat, a vivid glow,
In every crest and undertow.

Synchronicity defined,
Threads of fate in them entwined,
Ebb and flow in cosmic waltz,
Truths revealed in total halts.

In the quiet of the eve,
Shadows weave what we believe,
Through the vast and boundless skies,
Brilliant pulses never die.

Concerto of Concept

Thoughts compose a symphony,
In the halls of mystery,
Silent notes of wisdom ring,
In each mind, a song to sing.

Ideas float on winds of change,
In a range both vast and strange,
Melodies of insight bloom,
In the echoes, knowledge looms.

Harmony of fact and dream,
In tandem flows a ceaseless stream,
Concepts leap from mind to mind,
A concerto most divine.

Discord turns to unity,
In the quest for clarity,
In the end, it's truth we seek,
In every voice, a vision's peak.

Eureka Enclave

In the quiet of the night,
Flashes come of boundless light,
Moments of a whispered grace,
Eureka, truth in silent place.

Through the labyrinth of thought,
Gems of wisdom ever sought,
Glowing bright in mental caves,
Paths unknown through hidden waves.

Whispers in the void descend,
Guiding where the shadows bend,
In the sanctum of the mind,
Resolutions pure we find.

Revelations come to pass,
Mirrors vast in shards of glass,
In the silence, answers pave,
Journeys in Eureka's enclave.

A Symphony of Innovators

In gleaming halls where minds convene,
Ideas bloom, a vibrant sheen.
Voices meld in grand creation,
Sculpting dreams with dedication.

Whispers of invention rise,
Echoing through starry skies.
Passion fuels each bold endeavor,
Crafting legacies forever.

Tinkers, thinkers, visionaries,
Born from nights and sweet vagaries.
Together they compose the sound,
A symphony, boundless, unbound.

Every spark a note so sweet,
In a rhythm true, complete.
Innovation's pulsing heart,
Beats as one, a work of art.

Unified in quest and vision,
Boundless in their shared decision.
They create, as one, anew,
A symphony of dreams come true.

The Gathering of Ideas

Beneath the dome of endless skies,
Where thought and vision intertwine.
A canvas vast with bold designs,
Ideas gather, rise, align.

Here in realms of bright discourse,
Mind and spirit find their course.
Seeds of thought in fertile ground,
Grow in whispers, softly found.

Each mind a world rich and deep,
With secrets vast, their treasures keep.
Together they ignite the spark,
Illuminate the shadowed dark.

In circles wide, they share, reveal,
Bound by dreams, in common zeal.
Boundless in their quest for more,
Ideas merge and gently soar.

Gathered in this sacred space,
They chart the future's gentle grace.
Bound together, thoughts as one,
A tapestry of light begun.

Harmonizing Thought

Threads of thought, in harmony,
Weave a quilt of symphony.
Each note, each tone, each silent word,
In chorus loud, their truth is heard.

Minds converge in twilight glow,
Silken rivers, wisdom flows.
Bound by purpose, dreams align,
In perfect pitch, they intertwine.

Ideas rise like morning mist,
Catch the sun in golden twist.
Together as they brightly gleam,
A tapestry of hope they dream.

Harmonies of thought prevail,
Crafting futures, setting sail.
In unity, they chart the skies,
Wings of vision, hearts that rise.

Each idea a guiding star,
In the vastness, near and far.
They create a world anew,
In harmony, through and through.

The Fellowship of Vision

Beneath the ancient oaks they meet,
Where earth and sky in silence greet.
A fellowship of vision born,
To dream anew, each vibrant morn.

Eyes alight with future's glow,
In fellowship, their spirits flow.
Guided by the stars above,
A journey met with endless love.

Minds intertwined in common quest,
Hearts aligned and truly blessed.
With vision clear and purpose strong,
Together they both dream and song.

Through trials vast and shadows deep,
Their unity, a promise keep.
Bound by hope and visions bright,
They forge a path through darkest night.

A fellowship in purest form,
In vision bound, their hearts are warm.
Together they the world renew,
A tapestry in brightest hue.

United Conceptions

In thoughts, a single seed is sown,
Springing ideas long overgrown.
Dreams converging in one place,
Creating unity with grace.

Our minds like rivers intertwine,
Blending visions, so divine.
Shared imaginings, we conceive,
In togetherness, we believe.

A canvas vast, yet footprints small,
Collaborations build a wall.
Every stroke and every hue,
We paint with love, intent so true.

Melding spirits, blending hearts,
Crafting worlds as each part starts.
United conceptions take their flight,
In collective, boundless light.

Where pages empty, we inscribe,
The essence of a unified tribe.
Mosaic dreams to life, we bring,
In harmony, our voices sing.

The Assembly of Thoughts

Thoughts like stars illuminate the night,
Scattered fragments seeking light.
Gathered in a realm so vast,
United minds, a treasure amassed.

Ideas converge from every side,
In this meeting, none can hide.
Whispers turn to roaring streams,
Manifesting wider dreams.

Boundless echoes resonate,
Choruses that thoughts create.
Each assembly, each retold,
Shapes a tapestry uncontrolled.

Imagination's banquet spread,
Feasts of wisdom widely fed.
Every notion blended, sought,
In assembly of pure thought.

Together building, with delight,
Sculpting dawn from darkest night.
United, ever bold, we fight,
With thoughts assembled, futures bright.

Cohesive Brilliance

Shards of light, once broken glass,
Forge together, none surpassed.
Minds as one, in brilliance merge,
Creating sparks from every surge.

Ignite a beacon, shining through,
Brilliance formed within the crew.
Each idea a flickered flame,
Brightening paths with novel aim.

Effulgent glow from wise foresight,
Guiding stars in darkest night.
Interlaced and unified,
Brilliance, whole and magnified.

Patterns crossed, and colors wove,
Within a web of minds that strove.
Symphonies of intellect,
An orchestra of deep respect.

Togetherneath the light foresworn,
Brilliance from our union born.
A radiant whole, in harmony,
Crafting endless symphony.

The Fusion of Whimsy

Winds of fancy stir the air,
Playing tricks beyond compare.
In the fusion, colors blend,
Creating magic around each bend.

Whimsical whispers, secrets told,
Into the mix, imagination bold.
Boundless dreams, together spin,
A world where laughter will begin.

Colors swirl, a playful dance,
A fusion found in happenstance.
Smiles brought to life and form,
In whimsy, hearts forever warm.

Fantasy and reality collide,
Spreading joy so far and wide.
Every whim becomes a part
Of the fusion that's an art.

Join the merry masquerade,
Where whimsy's tapestry is made.
Fusion brings what none can see,
A world of endless jollity.

Fusion of Thought

Within the mind, ideas collide,
A dance of synapse, far and wide.
Invisible threads, they interlace,
Weaving a tapestry, mind's embrace.

From chaos springs a spark of light,
Illuminating depths of night.
Whispers of wisdom, ancient and true,
Reveal the paths the heart once knew.

Imagined realms where dreams resound,
In the symphony of thoughts unbound.
Infinite echoes of silent lore,
Unite the voices, evermore.

Concepts merge in radiant glow,
Creating worlds we long to know.
Beyond the veils, where doubts dissolve,
Find the truths that thoughts evolve.

Pioneers of Expression

In the quiet of a tender heart,
Words and visions take their start.
Courage found in lines of verse,
Pioneers, their thoughts converse.

Artful whispers in the night,
Signal dawn of endless light.
Carving trails through darkened skies,
Unlocking truths beyond the lies.

Voices rise, each unique and bold,
Stories of the young and old.
Expressions rich, a timeless flow,
Seeds of change in hearts they sow.

Bound by love, yet fiercely free,
Creators of their destiny.
In every stroke and every rhyme,
Pioneers transcend through time.

Radiant Euphoria

Beneath the sky of twilight hue,
Minds align in cosmic view.
In laughter's glow and joy's refrain,
We dance to rhythms, pure and sane.

Hearts unite in radiant beam,
A shared euphoria, lucid dream.
In moments brief, eternity found,
A symphony of life's sweet sound.

Each drop of rain, a crystal clear,
Enhancing moments we revere.
In the embrace of time and space,
Radiant joy in every trace.

Gazing in each other's eyes,
We find our truths where love lies.
A joyous burst, life amplified,
Euphoria, where souls collide.

Intricate Fusion

As threads of fate in patterns weave,
Complex tales we do conceive.
In harmony, the lines entwine,
Creating forms of grand design.

A dance of life, intricate, pure,
In each connection, we endure.
From fragments, whole emerges bright,
In every shadow, there is light.

Fusion born in silent thought,
Each unique, yet finely wrought.
Bound by forces, fierce and kind,
We shape anew with every mind.

Depths of being, complex and vast,
Reflect the future and the past.
In fusion, we discover grace,
A unity, a shared space.

The Concord of Ideas

Echoes of thought blend, aloud,
In chambers where minds explore,
Crafting visions of the crowd,
Innovations to adore.

Wisdom of ancient and new,
Harmonizing their bright rays,
A spectrum of each hue,
Guiding through daunting maize.

Symphonies of intellect,
Resound in whispered lore,
Ideas connect and intersect,
In minds that thirst for more.

Boundaries fade in the light,
Of creativity's dawn,
Together they ignite,
Concepts never withdrawn.

In the concord of ideas,
Unity finds its voice,
Through ingenuity's tears,
Together, they rejoice.

A Galaxy of Ingenuity

Starry thoughts paint the skies,
Each a beacon, bright and bold,
In the minds where dreams arise,
Blueprints for the as-yet untold.

Galaxies of invention gleam,
Through the vast expanse they fly,
Fueled by an endless stream,
Of visionaries reaching high.

Constellations of insight,
Guide the explorers' quest,
Finding new ways to unite,
From east journeys to the west.

Ideas orbit in grand parade,
Forming patterns, sparking flames,
By their light paths are made,
And no two thoughts the same.

Across the cosmic mind,
Ingenuity takes flight,
In the brilliance we find,
Inspiring the endless night.

Joined Innovators

Strangers in a common quest,
Seeking paths anew,
In the halls where ideas rest,
Gather minds that grew.

Through dialogues, they converge,
Bound by shared ambition,
Innovation as their urge,
With each new edition.

Thoughts entwine in joint resolve,
Passion in every thread,
In the labors, they involve,
With visions finely bred.

Strength lies in minds aligned,
Where creativity blossoms,
In the future they define,
Infinite, like the cosmos.

Joined innovators rise,
From concept to creation,
In the union, the prize,
Of boundless innovation.

A Union of Dreamers

Dreamers gather, spirits high,
In a realm where thoughts unite,
Building castles in the sky,
Fueled by imagination's light.

Visions merge, and dreams align,
In a tapestry of minds,
Together they define,
The future of all kinds.

Boundless in their shared ambition,
Test the limits of the known,
With each new proposition,
A foundation for the grown.

Their union forms a beacon,
In the ever-changing tide,
In dreams, they are not weakened,
With courage as their guide.

A union of dreamers bright,
In their fervor, we find hope,
For the dawn holds tight,
To the threads by which we cope.

Mingling Muses

In realms where dreams and daylight twine,
Muses mingle, whispers fine.
Their voices blend in twilight's gleam,
Weaving magic, gilding dream.

From ancient lore to modern plight,
They breathe in stars, exhale light.
With every verse, they paint the skies,
Crafting worlds where wonder lies.

Through the ages, hand in hand,
They summon stories, grand and grand.
Beneath the moon's soft, silver hue,
Inspiration's path they strew.

A dance of thought, a waltz of rhyme,
Eternal partners, endless time.
Their symphony forever glows,
In heart, the muse's river flows.

Envisioned Echoes

Echoes bounce through canyon walls,
Memories merge where twilight falls.
Envisioned dreams in shadows trace,
Reflections of an inner place.

Silent whispers, stories old,
In the air, their warmth unfold.
Timeless tales, both near and far,
Carried by a ghostly star.

Voices linger, soft and pure,
Marks of lives that were obscure.
In the silence, echoes breathe,
Weaving truth in hidden seethe.

In the heart, they find their nest,
Stories told with gentle zest.
Echoes sway in whispered breeze,
Timeless, lingering with ease.

Artful Anarchy

Canvas riots in vibrant storm,
Colors clash, reshape the norm.
Brushstrokes wild in fervent flight,
Chaos births a realm of light.

Fractured visions, broken chains,
Art transcends where passion reigns.
Every hue defies the frame,
Unleashing life's untamed flame.

Rhythms roar in daring flair,
Crafting worlds from boundless air.
Order crumbles, art prevails,
In anarchy, truth unveils.

Boundless minds in frenzied spree,
Create what is, what yet shall be.
In the chaos, beauty lies,
Artful anarchy, never dies.

Sculpting Stardust

In the silent, cosmic sea,
Stars are born in mystery.
Sculpting stardust, hands divine,
Crafting constellations fine.

Galaxies in grandeur spin,
Whispered tales from deep within.
Each a masterpiece of fire,
Woven by celestial lyre.

Through the void, they cast their light,
Patterns gleam in endless night.
Every spark a story told,
Of creation, brave and bold.

Sculptors of the universe,
Trace the ether, verse by verse.
In their hands, the starfields lie,
Dreams and wonders in the sky.

Harmonious Brilliance

In waves of sound, our spirits dance,
Under starlit skies, we find romance.
A melody that calms the night,
Guiding dreams, a tranquil light.

Notes that weave through hearts and minds,
In harmony, each soul finds.
A symphony of love and grace,
In every tune, a warm embrace.

With every chord, the shadows fade,
Lights of hope in darkness laid.
Together, we compose the song,
In unity, where we belong.

Echoes of the past align,
With present joys in time's design.
A radiant force in perfect score,
Harmonious brilliance forevermore.

The Nexus of Thought

Ideas bloom in endless streams,
In the nexus of our dreams.
Where wisdom meets the curious mind,
A tapestry of thoughts, intertwined.

Questions rise like morning mist,
In the labyrinth, we coexist.
Searching through the maze of doubt,
Until the light of truth comes out.

Each reflection, a star ignites,
Guiding us through sleepless nights.
In contemplation's silent grace,
We find our answers face to face.

Mind's horizon, vast and free,
In realms of pure philosophy.
Together, we uncover the plot,
In the nexus, each thought is caught.

A Choir of Creativity

Voices rise in colors bright,
In endless forms of pure delight.
Brush to canvas, pen to page,
Creativity takes center stage.

From whispered dreams, a vision grows,
In every heart, the spark that glows.
A chorus rich with boundless tunes,
Under the artist's many moons.

In rhythm, rhyme, and vivid hue,
Our essence forms the living view.
Through passion's lens, the world, refined,
A master's piece of heart and mind.

In unity, we craft the tale,
With every stroke, we set the sail.
A voyage through the soul's expanse,
A choir's song in every glance.

The Merger of Insight

Where wisdom's paths converge as one,
In twilight's glow, a new dawn begun.
Minds entwined, a shared delight,
In the sacred merger of insight.

Through shades of doubt, through veils of fear,
We find the truths that draw us near.
Each lesson learned, each bridge we cross,
Transforms us in the gain of loss.

In whispers soft and voices clear,
Knowledge binds us, soul to sphere.
In every gleaned and lit idea,
Life's grand mosaic, ever near.

With every thought, the bond grows tight,
In shadows cast by wisdom's light.
United in the quest we write,
Our story in the merger of insight.

Silent Symphony of Ideas

In the stillness, thoughts align,
Whispers of the bold, entwine.
Ephemeral sparks in twilight's hold,
A symphony of ideas, untold.

Echoes of forgotten lore,
Knocking on the mind's dark door.
Silent voices, ancient, clear,
Ideas bloom, transcending fear.

Dreams unite in silent dance,
Every notion, a chance for romance.
Minds converge, a cosmic sea,
A haven for creativity.

Sparks ignite in midnight's glow,
Eternal rivers, ideas flow.
Silent symphony, destiny's gaze,
Guiding minds through twilight's haze.

Whispers of Genius

In the quiet, brilliance brews,
Wisdom whispers ancient news.
Ideas burst, a starry flare,
Genius whispers through the air.

Silent moments, thoughts ignite,
Glimmering in the cloak of night.
A dance of neurons, bright, intense,
Whispers of genius, omnipresent.

Hidden truths, their veils unveil,
Bold discoveries set sail.
Every whisper, a new dawn,
Endless stars where dreams are drawn.

In the hushed twilight of the mind,
Genius whispers, true and kind.
Epiphanies in every breath,
Crafting wonders from life's depth.

Canvas of Dreams

Blank canvas, pure and bright,
Whispers tales through silent night.
Brushstrokes of the unseen,
Creating realms from the serene.

Colors merge in twilight's hand,
Dreams and visions, broad and grand.
Each stroke, a universe unfurls,
Infinite beauty, hidden pearls.

Images dance in moonlit beams,
Crafting art from midnight dreams.
Visions vast in every hue,
A canvas where dreams come true.

In the stillness, stories blend,
Wondrous realms, no end to end.
Canvas of dreams, unbound, free,
Art of life, eternal sea.

Choreographed Imagination

Mind's ballet, a dance unseen,
Choreographed in realms of dream.
Every thought, a graceful glide,
Imagination's boundless tide.

Steps of wonder, leaps of grace,
In the mind's vast, open space.
Choreography of the soul,
Imagined worlds, a lasting goal.

Silent rhythm, thoughts entwine,
Dreams and visions, sweet, divine.
Dance of muses, light and dark,
Imagination leaves its mark.

Twilight's stage, the mind performs,
Unseen dances, silent storms.
Imagination's grand display,
Choreographed in life's ballet.

Conjoined Imaginations

In the realm where thoughts align,
Our visions merge and intertwine,
A tapestry of shared design,
Imagination's grand combine.

We wander through the endless sea,
Dreaming far as eyes can see,
Together in this boundless spree,
Creating wonders, wild and free.

Our minds, a single, vibrant thread,
We walk where others dare to tread,
In a world by dreams we're led,
Where endless stories can be read.

Bound by thoughts, forever new,
Exploring vistas, bright and true,
In this dance of minds anew,
Conjoined imaginations flew.

Beyond the limits, past the skies,
Where every fancy freely flies,
Hand in hand, we realize,
The magic of our conjoined eyes.

The Joining of Dreams

In the quiet of the night,
When the stars are shining bright,
Two souls meet in soft twilight,
In dreams, they find their shared delight.

Through the fields of endless sleep,
Where the world feels wide and deep,
Their aspirations gently creep,
In unity, their hearts do leap.

Visions whisper, soft and light,
As they merge beneath the night,
Creating futures, pure and bright,
In the dreamland's sacred rite.

From hope's boundless reservoir,
They rise on wings to distant star,
Together, near or wildly far,
Their dreams are joined, a brilliant spar.

In the dawn, as shadows part,
They awaken, heart to heart,
Though the dreaming realms depart,
Their shared dreams, a work of art.

Melodic Ingenuity

Notes that dance upon the air,
Crafted with a tender care,
Melodies that we both share,
In a symphony so rare.

Harmonies that intertwine,
Echoes through a sacred shrine,
Our music forms a bright design,
With colors more than words define.

Instruments of thought and song,
Joining as we move along,
Each measure, neither right nor wrong,
A testament to bonds so strong.

Sounds that conjure vivid scenes,
Sweeping through our vibrant dreams,
In the flow of endless streams,
Where innovation reams and gleams.

Together we compose the night,
With notes of hope, and pure delight,
In this realm of sonic flight,
Our melodic ingenuity's light.

Shared Ambitions

With eyes set on a far-off place,
We march together in this race,
Ambitions shared, a steady pace,
Determination on each face.

Dreams that weave a common goal,
Together making us feel whole,
Day and night, our spirits roll,
Towards the vision in our soul.

Scaling mountains, crossing seas,
With a path that never flees,
In the wind, against the breeze,
Shared ambitions aim to please.

Hand in hand, we face the trials,
Through the long and winding miles,
With every step, our hope beguiles,
Turning hardships into smiles.

In the end, our dreams come true,
Crafted by the work we knew,
Shared ambitions, bold and true,
A journey that unites us, too.

Visionaries Emboldened

Hearts reach beyond the common sight,
A dream, a spark of brilliant light,
In shadows, courage claims its throne,
Visionaries, bold and fully grown.

With every step, a path revealed,
A future bright, once concealed,
Unfolding scenes of hope and grace,
Leading onward, finding place.

Through doubts and fears, they navigate,
Building worlds to innovate,
Seas of change they boldly sail,
Visionaries, they do not fail.

No longer bound by earthly chains,
Their spirits rise through joys and pains,
In every heart their fire sings,
Emboldened, they take wing.

So let us join with might and mind,
In every dream, our courage find,
Visionaries, hand in hand,
Together, conquer every land.

The Mingle of Minds

A sea of thoughts, a world untold,
In minds that meet, in hearts of gold,
Ideas blend like dawn and dusk,
In unity, we find our trust.

Monologues become a song,
Harmonies where we belong,
Through shared dreams, we create,
In the mingle, hearts relate.

Conversations flowing free,
An endless tapestry to see,
The beauty in collective streams,
Together, forging endless dreams.

Wisdom crossed, perspectives known,
Seeds of greatness widely sown,
In the mingling, life anew,
Creating wonders, we pursue.

Hand in hand, we intertwine,
In every thought, our spirits shine,
The mingle of minds, a boundless sky,
Where together, we can fly.

Collaborative Sparks

Flickers start in lone hearts,
Isolation gently parts,
When minds converge and souls ignite,
The world ignites, a beacon bright.

Through unified design and cheer,
Collaborations conquer fear,
Stars alight in tandem glow,
In concert, onward, spirits go.

Synergy weaves a bold embrace,
Tracing each ideal's face,
Glimmering through diverse thought,
Creating wonders dearly sought.

Building dreams with shared hands,
Together stronger, we withstand,
A spark of hope, a boundless stream,
Collaboration, life's grand scheme.

Sparks arise in union's gaze,
All together, hearts ablaze,
A brighter world, we all embark,
United in collaborative spark.

The United Blaze

In unity, a fire forged,
Souls and dreams in light converged,
A warmth that spreads through every face,
The world alight with a united blaze.

Through trials, tribulations spun,
Together, brighter as one sun,
A beacon shining, near and far,
Guiding hearts like a Northern star.

Strength in numbers, in spirit bold,
In the blaze, conviction told,
From every ember, greatness raised,
A tapestry of life, ablaze.

With hands entwined and spirits high,
Hearts ascend to touch the sky,
In unity, our paths unfazed,
The world transformed by our blaze.

Forever bonded, hearts intwined,
A future bright through collective mind,
In the flame, our journey's phase,
Together, we're a united blaze.

Dreamers in Harmony

In twilight's gentle whisper, we convene
Our dreams, like stars, in night serene
Bound by visions, across endless space
Together we seek, a destined place

Hope's soft melody, in hearts we find
Unity's chorus, through the binds
Luminous paths, we tread as one
Under the moon, till day is done

Threads of purpose, intertwine so tight
Dreamers uniting, hearts take flight
Harmony's gift, in each shared dream
Through twilight's veil, our spirits gleam

We craft tomorrow, with dreams anew
Sky-filled canvas, of golden hue
Hands clasped together, in this grand play
Harmony's dreamers, light the way

The Symphony of Thought

In the quiet of the mind, notes arise
A symphony of thought, under moonlit skies
Ideas like music, weave and twirl
In the silent dance, visions unfurl

Rhythms of wisdom, beat so light
Melodies of insight, guide through night
In each whisper of the soul, a tune
Harmonious strains, beneath the moon

Contemplative chords, in silence sway
Thoughts like an orchestra, night and day
In the concert hall, of the inner mind
Resonant echoes, intertwine

With each note, new thoughts commence
Symphonic journey, timeless and hence
In cerebral harmony, we create
A symphony of thought, intricate

Illuminated Journeys

Paths of light, in twilight's grip
Illuminated journeys, we equip
Stars as guides, across the night
Footsteps tender, hearts ignite

In the realm where shadows play
Light's gentle touch, shows the way
Journey together, yet paths unique
Toward horizons, dreams we seek

Lanterns aglow, with wisdom's fire
Guiding spirits, ever higher
Each step forward, illuminates
Journey profound, yet circumnavigates

In quest for truth, we embark
Illuminated journeys, ignite the spark
Light intertwined, with boundless grace
Together we walk, in luminous embrace

Together in Innovation

Boundless minds, in union soar
Innovation at the core
Ideas bloom, in fertile ground
Together in thought, we're unbound

Each spark ignites, a brilliant flame
Creative forces, none to tame
Collaborate in endless quest
Reach for the skies, do our best

Innovation thrives, where hearts conjoin
Shared visions, like stars they join
Discovery's path, we tread as one
Collective light, like morning sun

With hands entwined, we design
Future's canvas, dreams align
Together in innovation, we rise
Crafting wonders, beneath the skies

Shared Imaginings

In quiet whispers it begins,
The dream that binds us from within.
A realm where fantasies converge,
Across the skies our visions surge.

By starlit canvas thoughts are drawn,
A tapestry before the dawn.
In echoes pure, our voices meld,
In shared imaginings, we're held.

From heart to heart, the stories flow,
With threads of gold in evening's glow.
Enchantments woven, seamless, bright,
Together, we ignite the night.

Where wonder births, our spirits rise,
Creating worlds beneath wide skies.
With every thought, a new world springs,
In unity, our dreaming sings.

The Blend of Ingenuity

From minds unique, ideas bloom,
In every spark, dispelling gloom.
Innovation's light takes flight,
Transforming shadows into sight.

In brilliance pure, our thoughts combine,
Through alchemy of keen design.
Invention's marvels taking shape,
In unity, no dream escapes.

Each stroke of genius paints the air,
With colors rich beyond compare.
In symphony of bright intent,
Invention's path for us is bent.

Together we explore the new,
Where endless skies and dreams ensue.
With synergy, our essence true,
The blend of ingenuity breaks through.

The Convergence of Thought

Where minds converge, horizons gleam,
Connected by a common dream.
In unison, our visions soar,
To find what lies beyond the shore.

In sacred space where thoughts align,
We craft the future, line by line.
Through bonds unseen, yet deeply felt,
Our spirits merge, our fates are dealt.

With every word and every plan,
We sketch the endless span of man.
In thoughts we trust, we pave the way,
For dawns that break in bright array.

In synergy, we build anew,
From many minds, a single view.
Together, reaching heights unthought,
In the convergence of pure thought.

Luminaries in Concert

In harmony, the lights ignite,
A symphony of endless night.
Each star a note, each moon a chord,
In cosmic concert, dreams afford.

Celestial voices intertwine,
A chorus vast, both pure and fine.
Together, they compose the air,
A melody beyond compare.

As luminaries grace the sky,
In concert grand, they unify.
Through whispered winds and glowing beams,
They play the soundtrack of our dreams.

A celestial dance, a cosmic song,
Where harmonies of light belong.
In concert, they inspire all,
Luminaries, heed their call.

Effervescent Eclipses

In twilight's tender grasp, the shadows dance,
Above horizon's hem, they weave their trance.
Moons entwine in silent lover's meeting,
Their whispers echo, stars are fleeting.

Celestial blooms embroider velvet skies,
Glittering charms reflect in mortal eyes.
A cosmic kiss, where light and darkness blend,
In effervescent twilight, dreams ascend.

Nebulas blush in buttery hues,
As planetary orbs paint twilight's muse.
Ether's chill negotiates with morning's heat,
Each hour anew, with lunar rhythm's beat.

Gossamer veils of silver softly drift,
A night adorned in cosmos' gentle gift.
Effervescent fumes of comet's trail,
A symphony of light, in shadows pale.

Constellations whisper ancient tales,
As through the night, the wandering ship sails.
Effulgent beams in loops of time persist,
Effervescent eclipses in cosmic mist.

Nebula of Notions

In the quiet realms where thoughts disperse,
A nebula of notions turns and stirs.
Ideas like stars in clusters bright,
Illuminate the canvas of the night.

Woven webs of dreams and whispered plans,
Flowing freely from ethereal hands.
Within the mind's vast nebular expanse,
Each sparkle calls for reverie, a chance.

Imagination's galaxies unfold,
Stories glittering in radiant gold.
Before the eye they dance in spinning hue,
The infinite becomes tangibly true.

Waves of inspiration softly glide,
Through the currents of a cosmic tide.
Each whisper born a supernova bright,
Within this nebula of endless light.

Silent prophets in the dark expound,
Nebula of notions, thought unbound.
A universe within, uncharted space,
Endless realms of wonder to embrace.

Ingenious Interlude

In the pause between each spoken word,
In silence deep, true genius is stirred.
Where thoughts converge in tranquil solitude,
Emerges bright, an ingenious interlude.

Through quiet moments, insight softly gleams,
As moonlight shines on still and placid dreams.
A single breath, a pause to muse and brood,
Becomes the spark of an ingenious mood.

Sweet sonnets form in whispered ardent glow,
In this serene respite, the muses flow.
A brief interlude, with a touch profound,
Echoes creation in its fleeting sound.

Respite's charm in clever, silent sway,
Minds alight with thoughts in full array.
Within the heart, where stillness we intrude,
Is crafted there, this ingenious interlude.

The symphonies of thought here intertwine,
In moments fleeting, brilliant, and divine.
A silent burst of clarity renewed,
In this profound, ingenious interlude.

Whispers of Imagination

Softly spoken dreams cloud morning's edge,
Whispers of imagination gently pledge.
Sprouted from the seeds of hope and muse,
Each vision grows, where earthly paths bemuse.

Quiet voices sketch on twilight's shroud,
Pictures drawn from story's softest cloud.
Whispers weave through night's enraptured air,
Imagination breathes, a silent prayer.

Boundaries fade where fantasy begins,
Through whispered tones, the otherworld wins.
Ephemeral brushstrokes paint surreal tales,
In whispered hues, where vivid thought prevails.

Their murmurings ignite creative fire,
Whispers build each dream they do inspire.
Crafted realms from figments of the mind,
Imagination's whispers, unconfined.

In stillness, echoes come to life and play,
Whispers of imagination lead astray.
With deft caress, the mind unroots its chains,
In whispered realms, no vestige of remains.

A Fusion of Enterprising

In the heart of chance and choice,
Where dreams and deeds converge,
Ideas bloom with daring voice,
New realms of work emerge.

Risk and innovation streamed,
Paths unmarked and wide,
Every venture deeply dreamed,
With passion as the guide.

Markets pulse, and visions blend,
Commerce crafted, bright,
To the future they extend,
Crafted day and night.

Energies of mind and will,
Unified in scope,
Successes writ with iron quill,
On the scroll of hope.

Boldness cuts a twisting trail,
Where uncertainty's rife,
Enterprises vast set sail,
Charting modern life.

Pantheon of Thought

Among the realms of brilliant minds,
In halls where wisdom roars,
Visitors and greats entwined,
In endless mental stores.

Ancient voices, present day,
Ethereal meetings here,
Every spark a luminous ray,
Of insight crystal clear.

Ideas vast as oceans deep,
Their currents swift and strong,
They sail in dreams and hopes, to keep,
The world in learned song.

Eyes and ears forever keen,
To whispers on the air,
Knowledge stored, unseen, serene,
A place beyond compare.

Within this sacred thought domain,
In silent reverie,
Endless fields of knowledge gain,
A mind eternally.

Harmonious Insights

In silence, there the answers rest,
Within the quiet song,
The universe reveals its best,
As echoes blend along.

Enlightenment in humble chord,
Strums through the hearts of those,
Who seek the harmony award,
In symbiosis grows.

Wisdom hums in nature's beat,
Beneath both moon and sun,
Uniting thoughts where they meet,
In every mind and one.

Harmonious truths, entwined so fine,
Imparted with soft grace,
To see the world align in time,
In every sacred space.

From mind to soul, a gentle stream,
Insight flows serene,
Crafting life, a gentle dream,
In cues that lie between.

The Stratum of Brilliance

Beneath the surface, deep within,
A glint of genius lies,
Stratified through thought and kin,
A brilliance that defies.

Layered minds and wonders pure,
Enriched by questing hearts,
In every stratum, insight sure,
In every artful part.

Wisdom geode, uncracked, unseen,
A treasure yet to find,
The layers of the learned mean,
A glow within the mind.

From top to core, enchantment weaves,
An intellectual strand,
And through each mind, perception leaves,
A touch from nature's hand.

Oh, stratum vast and layer fair,
With brilliance ever bright,
May seekers delve and wonder there,
In everlasting light.

Collective Wonders

In the heart of unity's grace,
Where hands and hopes entwine,
Collective dreams find their place,
And possibilities shine.

Through shared voices, we sing,
A chorus of the bold,
In each laugh, in every spring,
Foundations of gold.

Strength in numbers, we hold tight,
Beneath a sky so grand,
Lighting up the darkest night,
Together as one band.

Paths converging with the dawn,
Unseen horizons greet,
In the march, both purposed and drawn,
Our spirits never defeat.

A canvas painted by us all,
With colors rich and true,
Collective wonders heed the call,
Together, we'll pull through.

The Tapestry of Genius

Threads of thought, finely spun,
Across the loom of time,
Wonders born when day is done,
And minds in rhythm rhyme.

From the sparks of knowledge's fire,
Ideas intertwine,
Crafted with unyielding desire,
Brilliance forms a line.

Every seam holds secrets dear,
Knots of wisdom's lore,
Patterns that to us appear,
Unlocking every door.

In the weave of every thread,
Colors rich and bright,
A tapestry of genius spread,
Revealing boundless light.

Through hands that craft and minds that dream,
A legacy our guide,
Genius flows in endless stream,
Woven with each stride.

Harmonized Prowess

In harmony, our strengths align,
Voices lift and wings unfold,
A symphony of hearts combine,
In courage fierce and bold.

Melodies of valor play,
In every whispered tone,
Together we shall find our way,
Where lesser souls bemoan.

Chords of passion resonate,
In the crucible of fate,
Through trials, we reincarnate,
And carve a brighter state.

With every skill and talent shared,
Boundaries dissolve,
In harmonized prowess declared,
Our spirits all evolve.

The song of unity persists,
Beyond the mountain's crest,
In every note, our will insists,
Together, we are blessed.

The Quilt of Ingenuity

Patches sewn with threads so fine,
Craft and skill unite,
A quilt where notions intertwine,
In day and through the night.

Each piece tells a story true,
Of minds that dared to dream,
Colors merging—old and new,
A visionary's gleam.

Ingenuity in every stitch,
Weaving tales untold,
Patterns rich, a treasure niche,
In fabric fold by fold.

The hands that craft, the hearts that lay,
Foundations strong and wide,
In every challenge on our way,
Ingenuity our guide.

Together we construct our art,
A legacy revered,
The quilt of minds and souls—our part,
A masterpiece endeared.

Orb of Inspiration

In the night's embrace, it glows.
Whispers of dreams, softly flows.
Guiding stars through twilight's veil,
A beacon where imaginations sail.

Embryos of thoughts take flight,
Sketching tales in moon's soft light.
Gleaming whispers, hope unfurls,
An orb that holds a thousand worlds.

Mystic dances in the air,
Colors swirl with utmost care.
Born from silence, pure and bright,
The spark ignites the poet's sight.

In the shade of cosmic tune,
Beneath the watchful, silver moon.
Seeds of wonder, deeply sown,
Inspiration's core, brightly shown.

Voices echo as they blend,
Celestial drops of light descend.
Captured dreams, on paper spilled,
The orb of muse, our souls fulfilled.

Tapestry of Insights

Threads of wisdom, gently weaved,
By the loom of truths perceived.
Patterns form in silken strands,
Guided by unseen, tender hands.

Echoes from the past align,
With whispers of a grand design.
Each moment, stitched with care,
An endless tale, beyond compare.

Colors merge, a vivid scene,
Illuminated by knowledge keen.
Contours of life's vast sight,
Woven through both day and night.

Lessons learned, forever bound,
In the fabric, truth is found.
A tapestry both old and new,
Each detail holds the universe’s view.

Wisdom's threads, both small and grand,
Craft a tale so richly spanned.
In this weave, our spirits rise,
A tapestry of age-old ties.

Revelation Rhythms

Beats of truth in shadow’s play,
Pulse of wisdom in the day.
Notes unveil the mysteries,
Through the song of histories.

Echoes in the valleys wide,
Secrets that the beats confide.
In every chord, a truth reveals,
The rhythm that our soul heals.

From the quiet to the loud,
Insights follow, proud and bowed.
In the cadence of the flows,
The heart of knowledge steadily grows.

Patterns shifting in the sound,
Revelations all around.
In the harmony of time,
We find the secrets so divine.

In the dance of every beat,
Wisdom's pathways we discreet.
A symphony of truth and might,
Revelation’s song in flight.

Symphony of Whim

Melodies born from the breeze,
Playful notes through willow trees.
Whispers of a fleeting rhyme,
Written in the sands of time.

Voices rise in joyous gleam,
Echoes of a whimsical dream.
Dancing through the corridors,
Laughter in the sound explores.

Fantastical, the notes unfold,
Stories of the brave and bold.
Orchestra of dreams takes wing,
In the symphony, the angels sing.

Rhythms of the light and free,
Carving out a destiny.
Born from whims of fleeting thought,
In the harmony we're caught.

Through the hallways of our minds,
Clever tunes and beats entwined.
Symphony of whim and play,
Guides us through each fervent day.

The Union of Creators

In shadows cast, new light begins,
United minds defy the winds.
A symphony of thoughts aligned,
Creation's tapestry unconfined.

Each brush, each note, each spoken word,
Crossing boundaries once unheard.
With hands locked tight, new worlds are formed,
A union bright, from chaos warmed.

Endless ideas, a boundless sea,
A horizon chasing destiny.
Harnessing stars in endless night,
Creators' hearts ignite the light.

Dreamers converge from distant lands,
Weaving wonders, no reprimands.
In harmony, their passions soar,
Creating realms forevermore.

A bond as strong as mountain stone,
Together, never walk alone.
From spark to flame, they rise above,
A union born of purest love.

A Cohort of Creatives

Gather round the table bright,
In the stillness of the night.
Voices merge in vivid hues,
Crafting dreams that we pursue.

Painted words on canvas steep,
Songs of oceans, mountains weep.
Imaginations intertwine,
In this cohort, lights combine.

Hands that mold the clay of time,
Breathless efforts, so sublime.
Emotion flows like rivers wide,
Brushing life where thoughts abide.

Past the bounds of finite fear,
With each notion drawing near.
From nothingness, they bring forth grace,
A cohort's art, in every place.

Tales emerge from hearts unbound,
A creative pulse, profound.
Together they birth stars anew,
A cohort of creatives true.

Brilliance in Tandem

Two minds converge, a fuse ignites,
Brilliance shines in endless nights.
In tandem, thoughts take flight and soar,
A cosmic dance, forevermore.

Words and colors intertwine,
In brilliance shared, a bound divine.
Unified, they break the mold,
Transforming whispers into gold.

As fingers trace creative paths,
Dual visions craft their aftermaths.
In tandem, hearts and hands unite,
A fusion born of sheer delight.

Energy, a boundless stream,
Flowing through a shared dream.
Crafting beauty, truth, and love,
Brilliance descends from realms above.

United quests of mind and soul,
In tandem, art becomes whole.
Together forging worlds so grand,
Brilliance marked by each hand.

The Commune of Thought

In cities built by shared beliefs,
In threads of hope, our hearts find relief.
The commune sings with whispered dreams,
In thought we weave our endless seams.

In circles drawn on earthen floors,
Ideas born as wisdom pours.
Voices rise in echoed prayer,
A commune bound by thoughts laid bare.

Hands that reach across divides,
In unity, our truth abides.
Through intellect, our spirits meld,
In this commune, love is held.

From mind to mind, a bridge we cast,
Transforming future from the past.
In every thought, a spark and flame,
A commune lives beyond a name.

Through dialogue, our souls ignite,
In shared visions, purest light.
Bound by dreams and knowledge sought,
We thrive within this commune of thought.

The Art of Collaboration

In the dance of minds we find our tune,
Ideas blooming like flowers in June,
Each thought a brushstroke on life's grand canvas,
Together we paint, with love as our compass.

The strength of many, a single force,
Navigating the challenges, altering course,
In harmony, we build dreams anew,
In every endeavor, rise as one crew.

From whispers of ideas, loud roars arise,
In shared endeavors, every heart flies,
Hand in hand, we conquer the unknown,
In unity, a masterpiece is shown.

Our hands entwined, we sculpt the clay,
Every challenge met, our fears allayed,
In tandem steps, a journey we chart,
Collaboration turns art into heart.

Through trials and joy, our voices blend,
In every storm, we find a friend,
Each effort combined, our spirits soar,
The art of collaboration, forevermore.

Minds in Melody

In the chorus of minds, melodies bloom,
Every note a thought, dispersing the gloom,
Harmonious whispers in the symphony of thought,
Each idea crafted, uniquely wrought.

Together we sing, creating a song,
In the melody of synergy, we belong,
A fusion of voices, gentle yet strong,
In every chorus, we find where we long.

Verses of wisdom, composed with care,
In life's grand orchestra, we share,
In every refrain, our spirits lift,
Minds in melody, the greatest gift.

Notes of brilliance in concert tend,
Every discord, a way we mend,
In the cadence of ideas, bound tight,
Minds in harmony, shining bright.

With every beat, the echo of souls,
Each collaboration shaping goals,
In the unity of sound, hearts rejoice,
Minds in melody, one voice.

The Fusion of Brilliance

When stars align in the night sky,
A brilliance born where minds comply,
Weaving dreams in the dark unknown,
Together, a light, brightly shown.

Each spark of thought, a guiding flare,
In the fusion of brilliance, ideas stare,
Across the horizon, visions meet,
In unity, our goals complete.

With intellect combined, mountains move,
In every challenge, expertise proves,
Innovation's child, born of minds entwined,
The brilliance within, perfectly aligned.

Radiance in thoughts, shining bright,
In the tapestry of ideas, pure delight,
Each thread of wisdom, finely spun,
The fusion of brilliance, all hearts won.

In the synergy of minds, a beacon glows,
Through trials and dreams, it grows,
Brilliance fused in every endeavor,
Illuminates the path, now and forever.

Unity in Inspiration

From the seed of thought, ideas rise,
In the garden of minds, where brilliance lies,
Each inspiration, a bloom in the sun,
In unity, our hearts become one.

The wellspring of dreams, boundless and free,
In every shared vision, a harmony,
Together we nurture, together we grow,
Unity in inspiration, all we know.

In the crucible of creation, sparks ignite,
In the fusion of minds, pure insight,
Every obstacle, a chance to inspire,
In unity, we fuel the fire.

Through the lens of hopes, we see anew,
In every shared moment, inspirations brew,
Hand in hand, we forge the light,
In unity, our spirits take flight.

With every heartbeat, a purpose defined,
In the collective soul, a tapestry entwined,
Inspiration's essence, forever found,
In unity, we stand, profound.

Wonders Embrace

In the twilight of dreams, we soar,
Beyond the realms, forevermore,
Through whispers of time, we trace,
The gentle touch of wonders' embrace.

Stars that shimmer, tales untold,
Mystic realms where futures unfold,
Paths of light, we daringly chase,
Lost in the spell of wonders' embrace.

Seas of cosmos, vast and grand,
Footsteps etched in unknown sand,
In every echo, a ghostly face,
Guides us through wonders' embrace.

Mountains whisper ancient lore,
Echoes ring from shore to shore,
With hearts kindled, we interlace,
Our shared dreams in wonders' embrace.

Through every tear and every smile,
We wander this enchanted mile,
Bound by time, in love's own grace,
We dwell forever in wonders' embrace.

Sunlit Scribbles

Morning light through window's pane,
Sketched in gold, a tender refrain,
In shadows cast, stories lie,
In sunlit scribbles, dreams fly high.

Whispers of dawn in hues so bright,
Eclipsing stars of silent night,
Each ray paints the sky azure,
In sunlit scribbles, truth is pure.

Words unspoken, dance on breeze,
In the rustle of the autumn leaves,
Tales of yore and futures free,
Sunlit scribbles hold the key.

On parchment bare, thoughts do bloom,
In morning's glow, dispel the gloom,
Lines of love in soft caress,
Sunlit scribbles, hearts express.

In every beam, a phrase untold,
Moments captured in sunlight's hold,
Through each verse, life’s glimmers trace,
Sunlit scribbles, gentle embrace.

Mindscape Mingle

Pathways carved in silent thought,
Dreams and fears by mind are wrought,
In shadows deep, ideas tingle,
In our endless mindscape mingle.

Echoes of old, futures unclear,
In the calm, and when storms rear,
Threads of fate begin to tangle,
Within the vast mindscape mingle.

Emotions flare, like stars they burn,
Questions rise, and then they churn,
Wisdom's whispers softly sprinkle,
Gems within our mindscape mingle.

We wander through our mental maze,
Lost in fog, or in bright blaze,
Veils of mystery past we dwindle,
In the swirling mindscape mingle.

In stillness found or chaos trove,
Depths unknown, we dare to rove,
In realms unseen, we gently dwindle,
Life unfolds where mindscape mingles.

Whirlwind Whispers

Breezes curl in twilight's sigh,
Mysteries swirl where breezes fly,
In the dance of evening's quivers,
Hear the silent whirlwind whispers.

Leaves that rustle, tales they weave,
Fates entwined, hearts that believe,
In the quiet, softly shivers,
Echoes of the whirlwind whispers.

Through the valleys and the peaks,
Secrets held by winds that speak,
In the night's embrace it lingers,
Glimmers of the whirlwind whispers.

Stories old in currents flow,
Wisdom of the winds doth show,
In its breath, both harsh and tender,
Timeless are the whirlwind whispers.

In the calm before the storm,
Voices faint but full of warmth,
Guides through life, with gentle flickers,
Pathways drawn by whirlwind whispers.

A United Mindscape

In the tapestry of collective dreams,
We weave a future that brightly gleams.
Threads of thought, so finely spun,
Bind our visions, one by one.

Through stormy nights and sunny days,
In unity, we chart our ways.
Hearts and minds, in perfect sync,
Shape horizons, on the brink.

Dreamers come from near and far,
Wishing on the same bright star.
Together, in this grand design,
Our spirits merge, our fates entwine.

Whispers turn to songs of hope,
In unity, we learn to cope.
Hand in hand, through time and space,
We build a future, full of grace.

A united mindscape, vast and free,
Where every soul can plainly see.
The strength found in our shared embrace,
Infinite as cosmic space.

Symphony of Innovators

Notes of genius fill the air,
Innovators, beyond compare.
Strings of thought, in harmony,
Compose a future, bold and free.

Brilliant minds, like sparks of light,
Illuminate the darkest night.
Through challenges, they carve the way,
A symphony in grand array.

Ideas dance, in perfect tune,
Underneath the silver moon.
Each invention, each bright spark,
Leaves a mark, a timeless arc.

Hands crafting, minds that dream,
Together form a flowing stream.
Progress flows, like rivers wide,
Innovative, side by side.

Melodies of change and growth,
A symphony that we both.
In concert, we perform our part,
Creating with a hopeful heart.

A Chorus of Thoughts

Thoughts arise, in choral splendor,
Whispering tales, both bold and tender.
In the silence, voices blend,
Ideas and dreams, without end.

Each mind contributes to the song,
In this chorus, we all belong.
Echoes of wisdom, rich and deep,
Through the ages, we will keep.

Visions shared, from soul to soul,
Create a harmony, strong and whole.
In unity, we find our strength,
Expanding thought, in breadth and length.

Words and musings, thoughts align,
In perfect rhythm, tales entwine.
Wisdom flows, like gentle streams,
Nurturing our hopes and dreams.

A chorus of thoughts, pure and bright,
Illuminates the darkest night.
Together, we can reach new heights,
In the symphony of shared insights.

The Conclave of Ideas

Gathered in a sacred space,
Ideas meet, face to face.
In conclave, minds convene,
Crafting visions, yet unseen.

Waves of thought, in ebb and flow,
In this circle, ideas grow.
From diverse seeds, insights bloom,
In the quiet, in the room.

Voices speak, in turns and rounds,
Each idea, meaning found.
Synergy of thoughts aligns,
Together, crafting new designs.

In the conclave, sparks ignite,
Creating pathways, shining bright.
Collaborations, rich and wise,
Unveil truths, that bind the skies.

Ideas flourish, take to flight,
In this sacred, shared light.
A conclave of minds, bold and free,
Crafting our shared destiny.

Spectrum of Thought

Ideas burst in vivid hue,
Across the mind's expanse so wide,
Silent whispers weaving through,
Colors in the brain confide.

From dawn till dusk they ebb and flow,
Shades of wisdom, light, and dark,
In the twilight thoughts aglow,
Painting bright the inner spark.

Rainbows form in moments fleeting,
Blending past with yet to be,
Imagination's heart is beating,
Pulsing with creativity.

Infinite the palette spins,
Mind's horizons stretched in flight,
Where one color's end begins,
Another dawns, anew in light.

Through the prism of perception,
Infinite our minds expand,
Fractals of introspection,
Colors weave a mental strand.

Echoes of Empathy

In the chambers, soft and deep,
Resonate the hearts unfurled,
Listening to the secrets keep,
A shared essence with the world.

Silent songs of joy and pain,
Reverberate in tender lines,
Connecting souls through invisible chain,
In the empathy of signs.

Gazes meet and feelings blend,
Without a word yet fully known,
In compassion's arms, we mend,
Healing hearts through gentle tone.

Mirrors of the self reflect,
Echoes tracing paths untread,
In each pulse we interconnect,
Bound by threads of what is said.

In the whispers of our care,
Mutual understanding thrives,
With each echo, love lays bare,
The common pulse in all our lives.

Chroma of Creation

In the universe's vast expanse,
Colors from a cosmic brush,
Every star and every glance,
A testament to nature's hush.

Palettes mix in nova's flare,
Fusion birthing light and hue,
Galaxies in beauty rare,
Painting skies in azure blue.

Planet's greens and oceans' depths,
Hues that tell a tale of growth,
In the twilight, sun's last breaths,
Crimson skies bind all in oath.

From the smallest bloom on earth,
To the farthest nebula,
In each line, creation's girth,
Colored with a true aura.

Every shade a verse composed,
In the symphony divine,
Art and science juxtaposed,
In each stroke, creation's sign.

Sanctuary of Thoughts

In the quiet of the mind,
Thoughts retreat to sacred space,
There the tumult left behind,
Peace and clarity embrace.

Sanctuary none may reach,
Save the self in introspection,
Voices whisper, soft to teach,
Paths to wisdom and reflection.

In the stillness, ideas grow,
Unfurling like the morning mist,
What was hidden, now to show,
In the silence, dreams persist.

Here the world cannot intrude,
Worries fade to distant shore,
In this mental solitude,
One can wander and explore.

Treasures found in thoughts so deep,
Glimmer in the mind's own light,
In this haven, secrets keep,
Guiding through the darkest night.

The Bond of Inspiration

Across the fields of boundless thought,
Where creativity's whispers weave,
A spark ignites, a vision caught,
Within the heart, we dare believe.

Linked by dreams that bridge the skies,
Through depths of night and morning light,
Together we let our spirits rise,
To turn the darkness into sight.

United minds, a tapestry,
Of endless hues and vibrant rays,
Conceiving worlds, so wild and free,
In eternal, fervent praise.

Our bond, an ever-flowing stream,
Of ideas pure and passions true,
We nurture every fleeting dream,
Until it forms, like morning dew.

From silent muses in the night,
To brilliant symphonies at dawn,
In inspiration's glowing light,
We find the strength to journey on.

Synapses in Sync

Electric pulses, thoughts align,
In neural dance, a rhythm found,
Connections spark in swift design,
As minds converge on common ground.

Through pathways rich with silent fire,
Each insight blooms, a flower's grace,
Our intellects, they never tire,
In this vast and intricate space.

The pattern flows from node to node,
In brilliant arcs of pure intent,
Ideas shared, their seeds bestowed,
In moments grand and eloquent.

In symphony, our minds compose,
A harmony of endless scope,
Where every spark and thought that flows,
Becomes a beacon of our hope.

In time and space, they intertwine,
These synapses of boundless wit,
Creating worlds where dreams define,
The endless realms where we commit.

Harmonized Genius

Within the void, a silent note,
Awakens worlds, yet undefined,
A synergy where dreams emote,
In harmony, our fates entwined.

Each genius voice, a ribbon bright,
That twines with wisdom's gentle hand,
We meld our visions in the light,
Of ideas bold and unplanned.

Together in a dance of thought,
Where intellect and passion meet,
Our minds unite in battles fought,
To forge creations rich and sweet.

In every chord of lullaby,
A whisper of the soul's desire,
Uniting hearts, we touch the sky,
With melodies that never tire.

Through trials faced and victories shared,
Our creativity, a spark,
In every moment deeply cared,
We find our light within the dark.

The Visionary Ensemble

Gathered minds with visions grand,
In unison, we boldly stride,
Through landscapes vast, a wondrous land,
Where every dream and thought collide.

Each voice a note in endless song,
Creating realms from phantom dust,
Together we, forever strong,
In our collective, boundless trust.

With brushes bold and canvases wide,
We paint tomorrow's boundless tales,
A tapestry where hope and pride,
In visionary light prevails.

Our minds, in perfect sync, align,
To shape a world both bright and new,
Where futures formed by our design,
Emerge like dawn from morning dew.

In every heartbeat, pulse, and breath,
Our essence flows, a river's sweep,
The visionary path we tread,
In dreams we share, and truths we keep.

Visionary Pulse

In the quiet of night, stars paint the sky,
Dreams ignite, soaring high.
Mirrors reflect our inner soul,
Where beauty blends, makes us whole.

A whisper of thoughts, a glimpse of light,
Gives birth to visions, in dark delight.
Nature sways with tender grace,
Imagination finds its own space.

Heartbeats sing a silent tune,
Beneath the silver, radiant moon.
Eyes perceive what lies beyond,
Mystical realms to correspond.

In each breath, in every beat,
Artistry and wonder meet.
Life's canvas vast and deep,
Through dreams, our spirits leap.

As dawn awakes, with colors bold,
New stories of the heart unfold.
Embrace the pulse that gives us sight,
For visions dance, in endless flight.

Maze of Inspiration

Wandering through paths unknown,
Ideas sprout, wildly grown.
Lost in thoughts, a twist and turn,
Inspiration's flame will burn.

Each corner hides a secret door,
To realms of wonder, and much more.
Shadows play, and whispers tell,
Of places where muses dwell.

Find your way, feel the spark,
Through the light and through the dark.
A journey carved, by dreams and ink,
Connections cross with every blink.

Footsteps echo, voices call,
In this maze, where musings fall.
Every pathway leads to new,
Visions waiting to debut.

As you tread this winding course,
Discover your creative source.
In the maze, just take a breath,
For inspiration defies death.

Luminous Abstractions

Colors swirl in midnight air,
Crafting dreams beyond compare.
Lights and shades in harmony,
Forming tales of mystery.

Shapes that float, designs so free,
Painting life's own tapestry.
Glow of dawn, and dusk's embrace,
Creates a space we all can trace.

Reflections dance upon the wall,
Silent whispers, none can stall.
Patterns fade, yet they persist,
In every hue, they coexist.

Candles flicker, casting forms,
In the wake of rising storms.
Glimmers, shadows intertwine,
In abstractions so divine.

In bright bursts and subtle gleams,
We find our most luminous dreams.
Hold on tight to every beam,
For light fuels the boldest scheme.

Echoes of Ingenuity

In whispers soft, ideas grow,
Like rivers with a gentle flow.
Echoes of thoughts, past and new,
Carve the path to what is true.

In the silence, voices rise,
Dreams unfold before our eyes.
Every echo holds a trace,
Of someone's brave, creative space.

Hands that mold and minds that dive,
Into depths where visions thrive.
Soundless songs of what could be,
Blossom into reality.

Bells of wisdom softly chime,
Marking moments lost in time.
Innovation's steady call,
Rises up, and conquers all.

Through the echoes, we shall hear,
Brilliance free from doubt or fear.
Creativity, a boundless sea,
Reflecting our ingenuity.

Emerald Epiphanies

In forests deep of emerald green,
Where light and shadow intertwine,
Epiphanies in whispers speak,
To hearts that on the leaves recline.

Beneath the canopy's embrace,
New thoughts like rivers gently flow,
The wisdom of the ancient trees,
In silent reverence, we know.

Lush secrets from the verdant hues,
Where flora's tales to us confide.
Roots grip the Earth and spirit's rise,
In nature’s boundless truths we bide.

The moss-clad stones, the fragrant pine,
As tranquil as a morning dew,
Reveal the epiphanies unseen,
In every shade and every hue.

Emerald realms, where dreams convene,
Epiphanies in green enshrined.
Within this splendor, subtle and keen,
Our souls and truths are intertwined.

Geniuses in Bloom

In gardens of uncharted thought,
Where seeds of brilliance begin,
A bloom of genius springs to life,
From fertile minds, a world within.

Each petal spins a tale untold,
Of innovation's daring flight,
Ideas unfold like morning's gold,
And pierce the veil of darkest night.

Flourishing in the gentle light,
Where curiosity takes its roam,
The blooms of genius shy from none,
In hallowed grounds of minds they home.

Such fertile grounds of pure insight,
With vibrant hues of audacious schemes,
The fragrances of future's hold,
Awaken vast and wondrous dreams.

Geniuses in bloom arise,
To paint the world with endless gleam.
Their essence, boundless as the skies,
Transforming thought into a dream.

Kaleidoscope of Thought

In twisting realms of colored glass,
Where prisms break the light anew,
A kaleidoscope of thought unfolds,
With insights bright and myriad hues.

Each turn and shift, a pattern wakes,
In endless forms of varied sight,
Perspectives twirl and interlace,
To forge a dance of luminous light.

In vibrant swirls of boundless glee,
Imagination takes its flight,
Exploring realms of what could be,
In every splash, in every height.

Ideas blend in vivid streams,
A symphony of form and grace,
In patterns rich, a world redeems,
A vision born in mirrored space.

Kaleidoscope of thought, divine,
Unlock the gates where dreams reside.
In brilliance, colors truth align,
And spread their wings, across the tide.

Printed in the USA
CPSIA information can be obtained
at www.ICGtesting.com
LVHW051634010824
787079LV00002B/163

9 789916 862476